LIFE CYCLES

The Life Cycle of Amphibians

Darlene R. Stille

Heinemann
LIBRARY

Chicago, Illinois

www.heinemannraintree.com
Visit our website to find out more information about Heinemann-Raintree books.

To order:
☎ Phone 888-454-2279
💻 Visit www.heinemannraintree.com to browse our catalog and order online.

Edited by Abby Colich, Megan Cotugno, and Kate deVilliers
Designed by Victoria Allen
Illustrated by Darren Lingard
Picture research by Ruth Blair
Originated by Capstone Global Library, Ltd.
Printed and bound in China by CTPS

14 13 12 11 10
10 9 8 7 6 5 4 3 2 1

Library of Congress Cataloging-in-Publication Data
 The life cycle of amphibians / Darlene Stille.
  p. cm.—(Life cycles)
 Includes bibliographical references and index.
 ISBN 978-1-4329-4978-5 (hc)—ISBN 978-1-4329-4985-3
(pb) 1. Amphibians—Life cycles—Juvenile literature. I. Title.
 QL644.2 .S753 2012
 597.8'156—dc22   2010038276

Acknowledgments
The author and publisher are grateful to the following for permission to reproduce copyright material: © Alamy: pp. 13 (© Robert HENNO); © Corbis: pp. 14 (© JAN-PETER KASPER/epa), 17 (© Raymond Gehman); © FLPA: p. 21 (Michael & Patricia Fogden/Minden Pictures); © Nature PL: pp. 10 (© Daniel Heuclin), 29 (© Hilary Jeffkins); © Photolibrary: pp. 15 (Animals Animals/Ted Levin), 20 (Peter Arnold Images/James Gerholdt), 22 (imagebroker.net/Franz Christoph Robiller), 23 (imagebroker.net/Justus de Cuveland), 25 (Best View Stock), 26 (imagebroker.net/Ingo Schulz), 27 (F1 Online/F Rauschenbach), 28 (Peter Arnold Images/Martin Harvey), 33 (Peter Arnold Images/Matt Meadows), 35 (Geoff Higgins), 38 (Anton Luhr), 39 (Animals Animals/David M Dennis), 41 (imagebroker.net/Alessandra Sarti); © Shutterstock: pp. 4 (© Maksimilian), 5 (© Jason Patrick Ross), 8 (© Jason Patrick Ross) ,12 (© mitzy), 16 (© Wolfgang Staib), 19 (© Dr. Morley Read), 31 (© guentermanaus), 32 (© Dan Lee), 37 (© Anyka), 40 (© Steve Byland).

Cover photograph of a red-eyed tree frog in Costa Rica reproduced with permission of © Corbis (© Paul Souders).

We would like to thank Dr. Michael Bright for his invaluable help in the preparation of this book.

Every effort has been made to contact copyright holders of any material reproduced in this book. Any omissions will be rectified in subsequent printings if notice is given to the publisher.

Disclaimer
All the Internet addresses (URLs) given in this book were valid at the time of going to press. However, due to the dynamic nature of the Internet, some addresses may have changed, or sites may have changed or ceased to exist since publication. While the author and publisher regret any inconvenience this may cause readers, no responsibility for any such changes can be accepted by either the author or the publisher.

Contents

Some words are shown in bold, **like this**. You can find out what they mean by looking in the glossary.

Look but don't touch: Many amphibians are easily hurt. If you see one in the wild, do not get too close to it. Look at it, but do not try to touch it!

What Is an Amphibian?

Frogs that swim in quiet ponds and toads that hide in dense forests belong to a special group of animals. This group is the amphibians. The word *amphibian* comes from Greek words that mean "double life." Most amphibians spend part of their life cycle as water animals and part as land animals. Salamanders and wormlike animals called caecilians are also amphibians.

A frog has bulging eyes, no tail, and long, strong back legs.

Cold-blooded vertebrates

All amphibians share other **traits**, or characteristics. Amphibians are cold-blooded. This means that their inner body temperature does not stay constant. They must warm their bodies in the Sun and cool them in the shade. Mammals and other warm-blooded animals can keep their inner body temperature about the same, even when it is hot or cold outside.

Amphibians are **vertebrates**, animals with a spine, or backbone. The backbone supports their bodies and helps vertebrates move. Animals without a backbone are called invertebrates. Sponges, jellyfish, mollusks, insects, and spiders are examples of invertebrates.

Metamorphosis

Most amphibians go through a process called **metamorphosis** during their life cycle. After they are born and as they grow up, their bodies take on new forms. They go through different stages. In the adult stage, many amphibians look totally different than they did during a younger stage. Young amphibians have **gills** for breathing underwater. Adults have **lungs** for breathing air.

Amphibians also have thin, smooth skin. They do not have feathers, hair, or scales.

A salamander has a slender body and looks a little like a lizard.

What Are the Different Kinds of Amphibians?

There are three groups of amphibians—frogs and toads, salamanders, and caecilians. Animals in the three groups look very different from one another.

Frogs

Adult frogs have flat heads, no neck, and no tail. They have four legs. Many frogs have **webbed** hind feet to help them swim when they are in water. On land, a frog uses its short front legs to prop up its body for sitting. Most frogs use their long, powerful back legs for making long jumps.

Most frogs are small animals. The biggest frog is the goliath frog. This frog lives in Africa. Its body grows to be about 30 centimeters (12 inches) long. Some of the smallest frogs known are about 1 centimeter (less than 0.5 inch) long.

Frogs have eyes that bulge out of their heads and let them see all around. They have smooth, moist skin. Their skin is usually green or brown, but some frogs are red, blue, or other bright colors.

Frog or Toad?

Toads are a type of frog. **Biologists** group true toads in the scientific family Bufonidae. True toads usually have shorter back legs and drier skin than frogs. Frogs have teeth and toads have none.

Toads

Toads look a lot like frogs. They are small animals without a tail. They are usually brown or gray. Unlike frogs, adult toads do not spend much time in water. They have dry skin that is covered in bumps called warts.

There are differences between frog and toad bodies.

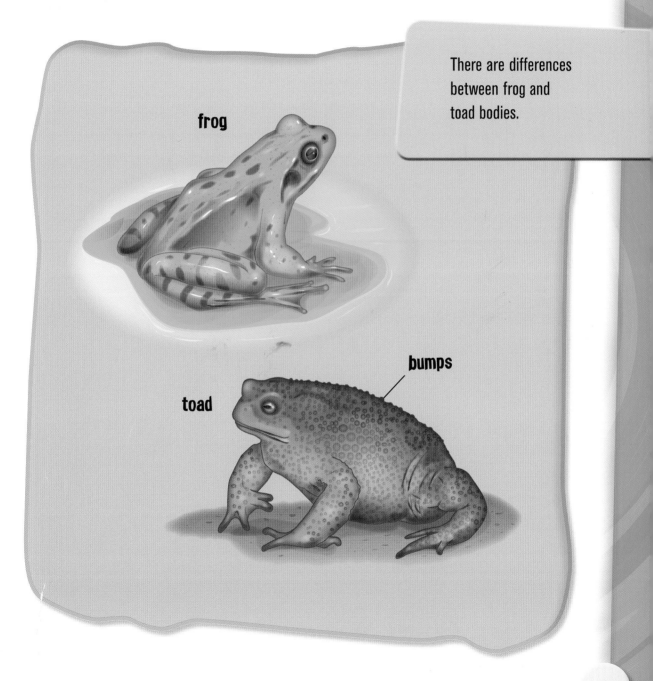

frog

bumps

toad

Salamander bodies

Salamanders look a bit like some lizards. They have slim bodies and long tails. Salamanders, however, are amphibians. They usually use their tails for swimming. They also use their tails for keeping their balance as they walk. They have smooth, moist skin. They do not have scales or claws as lizards do. Salamanders are shy, timid animals. They usually hide during the day and come out at night. They cannot harm people. Animals called newts and **mud puppies** are types of salamanders.

Most salamanders are small animals. Tiger salamanders of North America are usually 15 to 20 centimeters (6 to 8 inches) long. The common newt that lives in parts of Europe is 7 to 11 centimeters (2.8 to 4.3 inches) long. The biggest salamander, the Chinese giant salamander, can grow to about 1.8 meters (6 feet) long!

Salamanders usually live on land near water. Some salamanders spend most of their lives in water. Those that live on land have four legs. Ones that live in water may have only two legs.

The spotted salamander has dark skin covered with yellow spots.

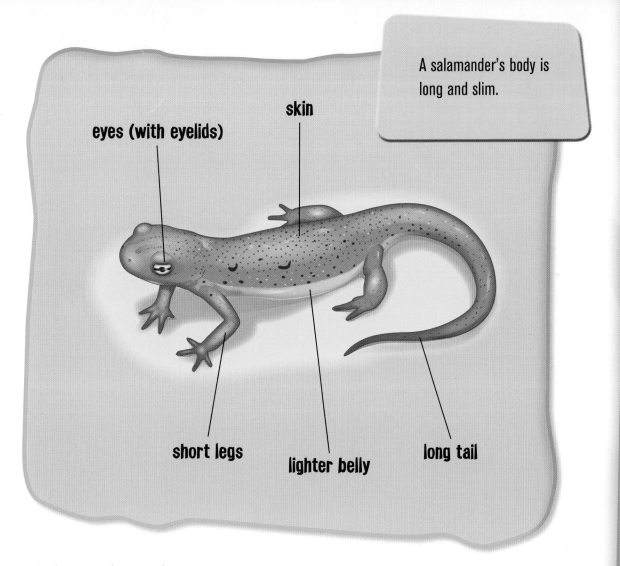

eyes (with eyelids)

skin

A salamander's body is long and slim.

short legs

lighter belly

long tail

Salamander colors

Some salamanders are dark brown, gray, or green. The dark colors help them blend in with their surroundings and hide. Mud puppies that spend their lives in rivers, ponds, and lakes have dark spots. The spots help them blend in with the sand, mud, and pebbles on the bottom. Most salamanders are brightly colored. Red salamanders are sometimes bright orange with black spots.

Wormlike caecilians

Caecilians look nothing like other amphibians. They have no legs. Small caecilians look like earthworms. Larger ones look like snakes. Some kinds of caecilians live in burrows underground. Some kinds live in water.

The head of a caecilian is hard and bony. It rams its head into soil to dig tunnels. Its jaws are lined with sharp teeth.

A caecilian has jaws lined with teeth.

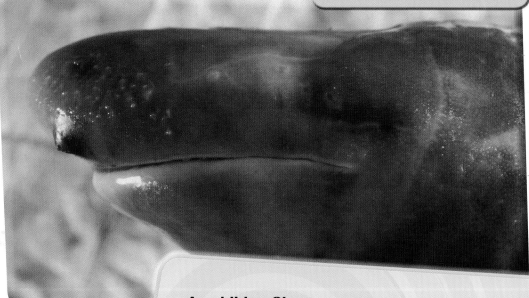

Amphibian Class

All amphibians belong to one big group called the animal kingdom. Within the kingdom, amphibians belong to a group called the phylum Chordata. Animals that share the **traits** of amphibians belong to a class called Amphibia. Different kinds of amphibians belong to groups called orders. Frogs and toads are in the order Anura. Salamanders belong to the order Caudata. Caecilians belong to the order Gymnophiona.

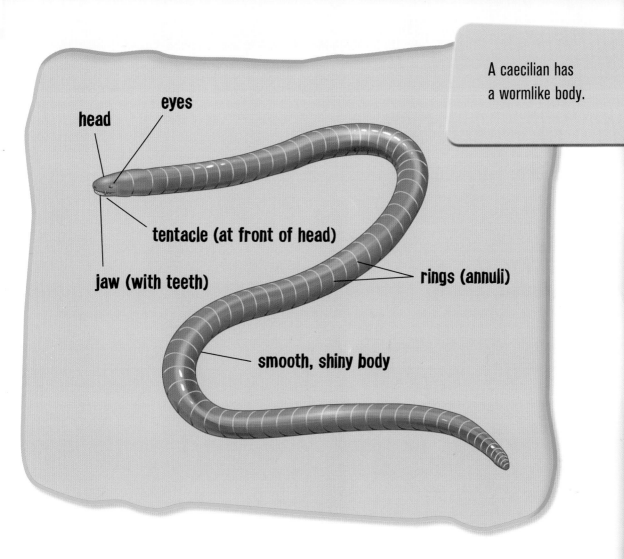

head

eyes

tentacle (at front of head)

jaw (with teeth)

rings (annuli)

smooth, shiny body

A caecilian has a wormlike body.

Caecilians do not have good eyesight. Some have tiny eyes in their heads. Others have skin over their eyes. Biologists do not think caecilians can hear very well, either. Instead of ears, they have **tentacles** on their heads that help them smell and locate **prey**.

A caecilian's skin is shiny and has folds that look like rings. Caecilians come in different colors, including brown, black, gray, orange, or yellow.

There are more than 170 kinds of caecilians. Some of them can be very long. The longest grow up to 1.5 meters (5 feet). The shortest are about 8.9 centimeters (3.5 inches).

How Are Amphibians Born?

Most amphibians begin life as an egg. The egg can be in water. It can be in wet, soggy ground. Many eggs never survive to **hatch**. Amphibian eggs are food for birds, fish, and other **predators**.

Tadpoles from eggs

Most frog eggs float in ponds or streams. Globs of what looks like jelly protect the frog eggs. The eggs look like tiny black dots inside the jellylike substance. The tiny dots grow bigger and bigger. They form heads and tails. Eventually they hatch by eating the egg around them. They go out into the water.

Newborn baby frogs are called tadpoles, or pollywogs. Tadpoles are the **larval** stage in the life cycle of a frog.

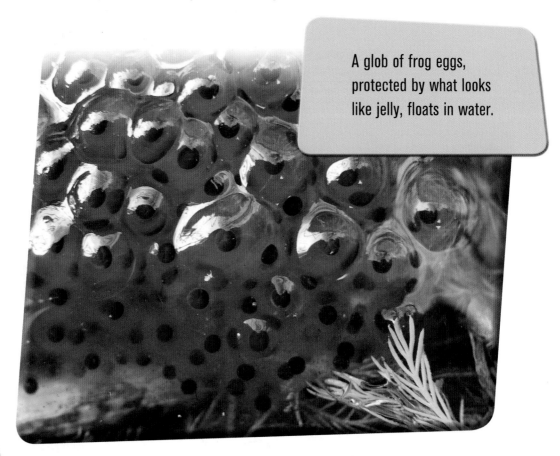

A glob of frog eggs, protected by what looks like jelly, floats in water.

The growing tadpoles look like tiny fish. They have **gills** for breathing. The gills take **oxygen** from the water. Tadpole heads are attached to one end of their bodies.

A tail grows from the other end. Tadpoles swish the tail back and forth to swim.

Toad tadpoles

Toads start from eggs just as frogs do. Long strands of jelly protect toad eggs. Often toad tadpoles hatch from eggs laid in pools made by spring rains.

Toad tadpoles must live in water. The tadpoles face many dangers. Other animals might eat them. They also will die if the pool of water dries up.

Predators, such as this great diving beetle **larva**, eat many frog tadpoles.

Salamander larvae

Salamanders hatch from eggs laid in water or on wet ground. Salamander females of different **species** have different ways of protecting their eggs. In some species, a poisonous jelly protects the eggs. Females of other species wrap each egg in leaves. A few salamander mothers stay around to guard the eggs until they hatch. Some mothers even keep the eggs in their bodies until the tadpoles hatch. Some lungless salamanders do not have a larval stage outside. They hatch right into small salamanders.

Most salamanders do have a larval stage. Salamander larvae look like adult salamanders with gills. Some salamander larvae have gills that look like feathers on the sides of their heads. They have tails, which they use for swimming.

Some caecilian mothers give birth to live young that have already gone through **metamorphosis**.

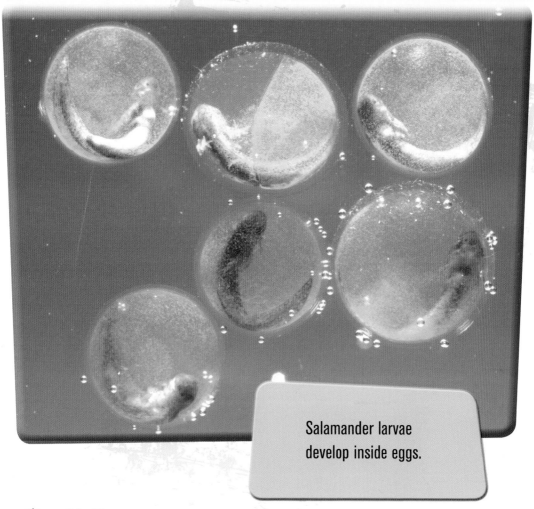

Salamander larvae develop inside eggs.

Caecilian births

Some caecilians hatch from eggs. Others are born live from the female's body. Caecilians that hatch come from eggs laid in damp holes close to water. When caecilians hatch, they become larvae. Caecilian larvae hide on land in daytime and wriggle into water at night. The larvae have gills for breathing and a finlike tail for swimming.

Like other amphibians, caecilians go through metamorphosis to change into their adult form. Young caecilians that are born live go through metamorphosis in the mother's body. Scientists know less about caecilians than any other amphibians. These creatures are very difficult to study because they live underground or in muddy water.

How Do Amphibians Grow?

As amphibians grow, they go through **metamorphosis**. Metamorphosis comes from a Greek word that means "to transform." Metamorphosis involves several stages in an animal's life cycle. The animal looks very different in each stage.

Changing stages

Animals other than amphibians go through metamorphosis. Insects such as houseflies, butterflies, and moths go through metamorphosis. Butterfly and moth **larvae** are caterpillars.

Most amphibians start to grow inside eggs. At this stage, the amphibians are called embryos. Next, they **hatch** into tadpoles or larvae. Tadpoles and most larvae live in water. They breathe with **gills**.

Frog tadpoles look somewhat like small fish as they swim by swishing their tails back and forth.

Becoming an adult

During the next stage of metamorphosis, the amphibians begin to change into adult form. They begin to look like small adult amphibians. Other changes also take place. The way they breathe changes, too. **Lungs** for taking **oxygen** from air replace gills for taking oxygen from water. The kind of food they eat also changes. Tadpoles and larvae usually eat plants. Adult amphibians usually eat animals.

Stages take time

Each stage lasts a different amount of time in different **species**. Eggs of some kinds of amphibians will hatch in a few days. Eggs of another kind may take several weeks. It takes tadpoles or larvae from a few weeks to more than a year to change into adult forms. Certain kinds of amphibians keep larval features all of their lives.

Tiger salamander larvae breathe through gills that look like feathers on their heads.

How tadpoles change

The change from a tadpole to a frog or toad is a metamorphosis. The change begins when back legs and front legs form. The body grows plump like the body of a frog or toad.

The tadpole's insides change, too. Lungs form and gills disappear. The stomach and other organs for digesting food change. The adult amphibian can eat animals instead of plants.

The young animal looks like a frog or toad with a long tail. The last step in the metamorphosis happens when the tail begins to disappear. When the tail is gone, the metamorphosis to frog or toad is complete. The frog leaves the water to live on land or stays in water. The toad leaves to live on land.

Very few of the tadpoles live to see the next stage. All kinds of animals eat tadpoles. Birds, turtles, snakes, and even large insects will eat tadpoles. The world is a dangerous place for amphibians in this stage of their life cycle.

Amphibians That Breathe Through Their Skin

All frogs and toads can breathe through their skin. Some amphibians have to breathe through their skin. They have no lungs. The best known of the skin breathers are the lungless salamanders. There are more than 370 species of lungless salamanders. They take in oxygen through their skin. They give off the waste product carbon dioxide through their skin, also.

During the metamorphosis from tadpole to adult, young frogs have both legs and tails.

How salamander larvae change

Different kinds of salamanders go through different kinds of metamorphosis. Most change into adults that live on land. Others change into adults that live in water.

The spotted salamander and other salamanders that live on land go through complete metamorphosis. The gills and fins disappear. They develop lungs for living on land.

Mud puppies, or water dogs, are one kind of salamander that lives in water. Mud puppy larvae go through a kind of metamorphosis. Mud puppies keep the large fins on their tails. They develop lungs, but they keep their feathery, reddish gills for living in water.

The time it takes salamanders to finish metamorphosis depends on the species. Some become adults in a few months. It takes the mud puppy up to five years.

Mexican Axolotl

This salamander never quite grows up. The axolotl goes through an incomplete metamorphosis. It keeps its fins and feathery gills for living in water. It does develop sex organs so that it can **reproduce**.

Salamander larvae have frilly gills.

A caecilian gives birth to live young.

Caecilian metamorphosis

Larvae of **oviparous** caecilians that hatch from eggs have gills and fins. They change into adults that can live on land. They lose their gills. They develop one lung, thicker skin, and **tentacles**.

Viviparous caecilians are born live. They go through metamorphosis in the body of their mother. They come out looking like small adult caecilians. Many live in water.

How Do Amphibians Move Around?

Amphibians have different ways of moving in different stages of their life cycle. As adults, some move better on land and some in water.

Larvae swim

Most amphibian **larvae** live in water. The tadpoles of frogs and toads look like fish. They have no legs. They have fins on their tails for swimming. Salamander larvae look more like little salamanders with tiny legs. They also have fins on their tails for swimming, while they live in water. Caecilian larvae have tails with fins for swimming.

Toads have weaker back legs than frogs, so they do not jump or swim as well.

Frogs leap and swim

Adult frogs use their strong back legs to make long leaps. Most frogs can jump about 10 times the length of their bodies. Australia's rocket frog, which is about 1 centimeter (less than 0.5 inch) long, can leap about 55 times the length of its body!

Adult frogs that live around water can swim. They have **webbed** feet for paddling around in water. One kind of frog can even "fly." Flying tree frogs use the large webbing on their feet to glide from branch to branch in tropical rain forests.

Toads walk

Toads have shorter back legs than frogs do. Toads use their legs more for walking than for jumping. Spadefoot toads have hard claws on their back feet. They use these **"spades"** to dig burrows in dry, hot soil.

A frog uses its webbed back feet as "swim fins" to move easily in water.

Salamanders swim and walk

Like other amphibian larvae, salamander larvae get around by swimming. Like tadpoles, they use fins on their tails to move through water.

Adult salamanders keep their tails. They use their tails for swimming when they go into water. Most have four legs for walking on land. Salamanders that live mainly in water may only have two legs. Some salamanders can climb. The arboreal salamander has special toe pads on its feet. The toe pads are an **adaptation** for living in and climbing around trees.

Caecilians slither

The long, legless bodies of caecilians are made for pushing through underground tunnels. In order to move, these amphibians must dig the tunnels. A caecilian braces the back part of its body on the tunnel wall. Then it rams its hard head into the soil in front. Ramming pushes the soil away and makes the tunnel longer.

Studying Caecilians

Few people have ever seen a caecilian. Because they live underground, they are difficult for scientists to study. One scientist put a caecilian in a clear, plastic tube. He filled a part of the tube with soil. He studied how the caecilian moves and digs through soil. Because caecilians have poor eyesight, they did not know when they were being watched. A British filmmaking crew built a movie set that looked like the tunnels caecilians live in. The set had clear walls so that the crew could film the wormlike amphibians.

The Chinese salamander, one of the world's largest **species**, has a broad, flat body for swimming on the bottom of shallow streams.

What Do Amphibians Eat?

The kind of food an amphibian eats depends on the stage of its life cycle. Newborn tadpoles are mainly **herbivores**. Herbivores eat plants. Older tadpoles and adults are mainly **carnivores**. Carnivores eat meat. Salamanders and caecilians eat other animals in all life cycle stages.

Tadpoles graze

Tadpoles of frogs and toads **hatch** with a **yolk sac** attached to their bodies. They feed off the yolk sac for the first few days. When they use up the yolk sac, the tadpoles eat **algae** and water plants.

Tadpoles have a beak like that of a parrot. They also have a round mouth like a disk. Inside the mouth are several rows of teeth. The tadpole uses its mouth to grab onto algae. Its beak bites off pieces of algae. The rows of teeth scrape algae off of rocks or other surfaces.

A tadpole scrapes algae
from water plants or rocks.

This frog attempts to catch its prey.

Salamander larvae

Like tadpoles, newly hatched salamander **larvae** have a yolk sac. They use their yolk sac for food until they are big enough to eat. The larvae then start to eat tiny animals, such as the larvae of insects. Salamander larvae do not eat plants.

Caecilian food

Caecilians are carnivores. Because they are difficult to study, scientists do not know for sure what kind of food caecilian larvae eat. They think they eat larvae and tiny water animals. Small adult caecilians eat insects and worms. Big caecilians may eat small lizards and small mammals, such as mice.

Food for frogs and toads

Adult frogs and toads eat all kinds of animals. Frogs and toads that live on land eat insects, **grubs**, slugs, earthworms, and spiders. Frogs and toads can sense the movement of **prey**. Frogs use their bulging eyes to detect movement in all directions.

Neither frogs nor toads chew their food. Toads have no teeth. Some frogs only have upper teeth. These amphibians swallow their food whole.

Some frogs and toads have long tongues with sticky ends. Frogs and toads flick out their long, sticky tongues to catch insects and spiders.

Big bullfrogs will eat anything small enough for them to swallow. In water they catch small fish, such as minnows, crayfish, and the tadpoles of other amphibians. On land, they eat insects such as crickets and termites, small birds, and even mice.

The giant bullfrog has a diverse diet.

The young of a caecilian **species** that lives in Africa eat their mother's skin.

Salamander dinners

Adult salamanders that live on land eat worms, centipedes, crickets, spiders, earthworms, slugs, and bugs. **Mud puppies** and other salamanders that live in water eat fish eggs, crayfish, leeches, and larvae of other amphibians.

Some salamanders, such as the tiger salamander, capture prey by quickly snapping their jaws shut. Others, such as lungless salamanders, have tongues that they can shoot out to grab worms and insects.

Salamanders have upper and lower teeth. They do not use their teeth for chewing. They use their teeth for holding their prey.

Where Do Amphibians Live?

Amphibians live on all **continents** except Antarctica. Antarctica is the continent around the South Pole.

Tropical amphibians

Biologists think there are at least 6,500 **species** of amphibians. Most amphibian species live in tropical areas near the equator. The equator is an imaginary line that divides Earth into northern and southern halves. The climate near the equator is warm all year long. The farther north or south of the equator you go, the colder the climate becomes. It is cold all year long at the north and south poles.

There are so many amphibians in the tropics because these animals are cold-blooded. When the temperature outside is hot, the amphibian's body heats up. When the temperature outside is cold, the amphibian's body gets cold. In the warm tropics, life is easier for cold-blooded amphibians.

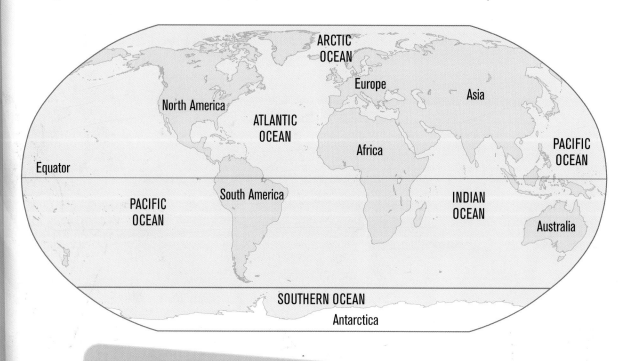

Amphibians live on all continents except Antarctica.

Endangered Amphibians

More than 160 amphibian species have gone **extinct** since the 1980s. About one-third of amphibian species are threatened with extinction. One cause is infection with a skin fungus. Damaged amphibian skin grows back thicker. The thicker skin can't exchange gases or absorb water very well.

Destruction of tropical forest is another cause. Amphibians lose their **habitats**, or natural homes. Amphibians also suffer when new animals come into an area. They compete with the local amphibians for food. Pollution is another problem affecting amphibians. In 2005 scientists all over the world came up with a plan to save amphibians. It includes **breeding** endangered amphibians in zoos and returning them to their natural homes.

Local homes

The natural home areas of animals are called habitats. Most amphibians live in habitats that are damp because their skin needs to be moist. They live in areas close to lakes, streams, ponds, and rivers.

Caecilians only live underground or in water in tropical habitats. Different species live in Africa, South America, and Asia.

Some amphibians live in dry habitats. Red-spotted toads live near streams in desert areas of the southwestern United States and northern Mexico. Even if these toads lose almost half the water in their bodies, they can live. During dry times, the skin of this toad can take up water in the form of **dew**.

The red-eyed tree frog of South America has suction cups on its toes to help it climb trees.

Coping with seasons

Some amphibians live in climates with four seasons. Summers are hot and winters are cold. When it is cold, amphibians go into a sleeplike state called **hibernation**. Some frogs hibernate at the bottom of pools or streams. Their skin takes in **oxygen** from the water. Some frogs and toads dig holes in the ground and live off fat and sugar in their bodies.

Tropical areas and deserts have dry and rainy seasons. Some amphibians, such as the California tiger salamander, go underground to survive hot, dry times. They find or dig burrows and go into a sleeplike state called **estivation** until rain comes.

The marbled salamander often lives under rotting logs in swamps.

How Do Amphibians Spend Their Time?

Amphibians spend a lot of time getting food, eating food, and resting. Some amphibians are out and about during the day. Others are "night owls" that sleep and hide during the day. They look for food and eat at night.

Ambush experts

Most amphibians do not hunt for food. They wait for food to come to them. They sit still and ambush their **prey**. When a worm or insect comes along, the amphibian nabs it. A frog or toad shoots out a sticky tongue. Some salamanders snap their jaws around prey and swallow it. Other salamanders and caecilians come across dinner while crawling, swimming, or walking. They might find a tasty earthworm or insect and swallow it.

Amphibian "Antifreeze"
Wood frogs can live north of the Arctic Circle. In winter, wood frogs become frozen "frogsicles." Other amphibians, such as the Siberian salamander of northern Russia, can also freeze and thaw. They have a chemical in their blood that allows them to freeze and thaw out again. The chemical keeps ice from forming in their cells.

Resting and hibernating

Frogs and toads sometimes sit still. They close their eyes. Scientists are not sure whether the amphibians are just resting or sleeping.

In cold or hot, dry climates, amphibians can spend months **hibernating** or **estivating**. Some frogs that estivate shed outer layers of their skin and wrap themselves up in them. This helps keep their skin stay moist while they estivate for weeks or months.

A frog rests with its eyes closed.

How Do Amphibians Protect Themselves?

Amphibians have many **predators**. Birds, raccoons, turtles, and snakes are some of the animals that **prey** on amphibians. Amphibians can't give a poisonous bite, but they have developed other ways of protecting themselves.

Hiding and blending in

Salamanders try to stay out of the way of enemies. They hide under leaves or fallen logs. Caecilians burrow under the ground and stay very well hidden.

Frogs and toads sometimes hide in plain sight by blending in with their surroundings. Tree frogs are green and blend in with leaves. Many toads are brown or gray. Sometimes toad skin has patterns that look like pebbles or dead leaves.

Blowgun Darts

Since ancient times, native people of South America have used poison dart frogs for hunting. They dipped darts for their blowguns in poison from the skin of the poison dart frog. Many kinds of animals die from the poison.

Scary colors and poisonous creatures

Some amphibians are brightly colored. Their colors could be a warning to predators. Some frogs, toads, and salamanders give off liquids that are poisonous to animals that attack them.

Poison dart frogs have skin glands that give off the most powerful poisons. There are about 200 **species** of these frogs. They come in blues, reds, and other colors.

The red-eyed tree frog can hide in rain forest trees because it is green. It can also flash its blue legs and red eyes if attacked. The sudden show of colors can scare predators away.

The poison dart frog has brightly colored skin.

How Do Amphibians Have Babies?

All amphibians **reproduce** sexually. Sperm from a male **fertilizes** eggs from a female.

Mating in water

Almost all amphibians mate in water. They usually return every year to the same pond, lake, river, or stream. They typically mate during a rainy time of year. In North America and Europe, they mate in spring.

When it is time to mate, large numbers of amphibians gather in or near a body of water. They choose partners. Mating takes place at night.

A male Luristan newt performs his courtship dance for a female.

Salamander courtship dance

Most salamanders do a courtship "dance" before mating. Red salamanders do a typical dance. The male red salamander rubs his nose on the female's head. She later puts her head on his tail. Other salamander dances include biting and head touching.

After dancing, salamander males leave a jellylike packet of sperm called a spermatophore. The females pick up the spermatophores. They use the sperm to fertilize eggs inside their bodies. Salamanders are **oviparous.** The females lay their eggs in the water or on wet ground. The eggs are not inside a hard shell. They are in a mass of jelly. The females often stay around to guard the eggs from being eaten by fish and other amphibians.

Different kinds of salamanders lay varying numbers of eggs. The small-mouthed salamander lays as few as six at a time. The hellbender lays up to 400!

A female salamander lays a jellylike mass of eggs in water.

Frog mating calls

Most frogs mate in water. Frogs mate during the rainy season in the tropics. They mate during spring in climates with four seasons.

Males enter the water first. They call to females. Each **species** of frog has its own mating call. To make this sound, a male frog pushes air through his vocal cords into a vocal **sac**. The vocal sac is a pouch that can be under his mouth or at the sides of his mouth. The vocal cords vibrate to make the sound. The vocal sac makes the mating call sound louder.

When a female comes to a male frog, the male takes hold of her back. The female frog sends eggs into the water. The male fertilizes the eggs as they leave her body. Frogs are oviparous. Some frogs lay thousands of eggs at a time. Frog eggs do not have shells. They are covered in a jelly.

A male frog uses his vocal sac to make loud mating calls.

A male frog fertilizes eggs as a female sends them into the water.

Toad mating

Toads mate in ways that are a lot like frogs. Adult toads live on land. They mate in water.

Most male toads have mating calls to attract females. They fertilize eggs as the female sends them into the water. Toads are oviparous. A female may lay up to 30,000 eggs at a time! Toads mate in the spring when the weather is rainy. The rain makes shallow pools of water that later dry up. Toads mate in these pools.

How caecilians breed

Caecilians give birth in two ways. Some are oviparous. They lay eggs. Some are **viviparous**. They give birth to live young.

All male caecilians fertilize eggs with sperm in the female's body. Some oviparous caecilians lay the fertilized eggs in water. Others lay their fertilized eggs on land.

Caecilian eggs laid in water **hatch** into **larvae** that grow up in water. Those that hatch from eggs laid on land and those born live do not go through a larval stage outside the egg.

Amphibian ages

Some kinds of amphibians live longer than others. Scientists mainly know about amphibians living in captivity. They believe that amphibians in the wild do not live as long as those in zoos or kept as pets.

Frogs and toads in captivity usually live from 4 to 15 years. The oldest living toad may be a common toad that lived for 40 years.

Some salamanders can live a long time. Tiger salamanders can live up to 25 years. There is a Japanese fire belly newt that is more than 27 years old, and an eastern newt that has lived for 20 years.

No one has any idea how long caecilians live. So few caecilians have ever been seen, let alone studied.

The life cycle of most amphibians begins with an egg. The egg hatches and develops into a larva that goes through **metamorphosis**. It changes into a totally different adult form that can reproduce and make more amphibians.

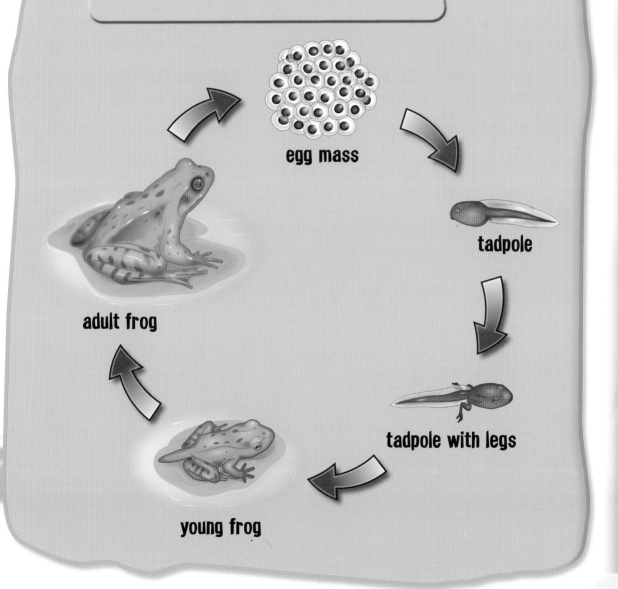

egg mass

tadpole

tadpole with legs

young frog

adult frog

Amphibian Facts

Amphibians first appeared on Earth about 360 million years ago.

Brazil has about 800 known amphibian **species**—more than any other country.

Tree frogs lay eggs on the underside of a leaf hanging over water. When the tadpoles **hatch**, they tumble from the leaf into the water.

There are more species of frogs than any other kind of amphibian. Of some 6,200 kinds of amphibians, more than 4,000 are frogs and toads.

The Siberian salamander can live in temperatures as low as -56°C (-69°F).

Frogs have many taste buds in their mouths and will spit out any food that tastes bad to them.

The Australian water-holding frog fills its body with water and wraps itself tightly in skin that it has shed. Buried in mud, this frog can live without water in a dry part of Australia for about two years.

Each species of frog has its own mating call. A female frog only goes to male frogs making the call of her species.

The male Darwin's frog carries developing tadpoles in its vocal **sac** until they develop into froglets.

A mass of frog eggs protected in jelly is called frogspawn.

Some female salamanders that lay their eggs on land guard the eggs for several months until they hatch. During this time, called brooding, the mother might not eat or might only eat very little.

All newts are salamanders, but all salamanders are not newts. Newts are salamanders that live mainly on land rather than water.

A siren is a salamander that never quite grew up. It stopped developing in the **larval** stage and has both **gills** and **lungs** for breathing.

Glossary

adaptation a change that makes a species better suited to its environment

alga (pl. algae) small plant or plantlike organism

biologist scientist who studies living things

breed to produce offspring

carnivore meat eater

continent large mass of land

dew small drop of moisture that forms on cool surfaces at night

estivation sleeplike state in which animals spend hot, dry summers

extinct no longer in existence

fertilize joining of egg and sperm to produce a new animal

gill organ for getting oxygen out of water

grub insect larva

habitat natural home of a plant or animal

hatch break out of an egg

herbivore plant eater

hibernate go into a sleeplike state in which an animal spends the winter

larva (pl. larvae) early form of an organism that comes after the egg stage

larval stage in the life cycle of an organism when it is a larva

lung organ that supplies the blood with oxygen and gets rid of carbon dioxide

metamorphosis change in form of some creatures as they grow

mud puppy type of salamander with gills that lives in water

oviparous giving birth to young by laying eggs that hatch

oxygen gas in the air that is needed for animal life

predator animal that hunts another animal

prey animal that is hunted and killed for food by another animal; to hunt another animal

reproduce to produce offspring

sac bag or pouch

spade digging tool that is like a shovel

species group of similar organisms

tentacle thin body part on the head of some animals used for grasping or sensing

trait feature or quality of an organism

vertebrate animal with a backbone

viviparous giving birth to live young that develop inside the mother's body

webbed having a flap of skin between the toes

yolk part of an egg that provides food for the embryo

Find Out More

Books

Allen, Kathy. *Deformed Frogs: A Cause and Effect Investigation*. Mankato, Minn.: Capstone, 2011.

Bailer, Darice. *How Do Tadpoles Become Frogs?* New York: Marshall Cavendish Benchmark, 2010.

Ganeri, Anita. *Poison Dart Frog*. Chicago: Heinemann Library, 2011.

Lundgren, Julie K. *Frogs and Toads*. Vero Beach, Fla.: Rourke, 2011.

Nelson, Robin. *Salamanders*. Minneapolis: Lerner, 2009.

Websites

All About Frogs
http://allaboutfrogs.org

Frogs of Borneo
www.frogsofborneo.org

National Geographic Kids: Creature Features
http://kids.nationalgeographic.com/kids/animals/creaturefeature

Smithsonian National Zoological Park: Reptiles & Amphibians
http://nationalzoo.si.edu/Animals/ReptilesAmphibians/ForKids/default.cfm

Index